SMOOTHIES RECIPES FOR WEIGHT GAIN

Unlock the Secret to Gaining Healthy Weight with Delicious and Nutrient Packed Smoothies

4-Week Smoothie Weight Gain Meal Plan

&

4-Week Weight Gain Exercise Plan

KARIE BISHOP

1

It is important to note that the information in this book is for educational and informational purposes only. Karie Bishop is not a licensed healthcare professional or a registered dietitian, so the content of this book should not be considered as medical or professional advice. The suggestions, recipes and strategies outlined in this book are based on the author's personal experiences, research and general knowledge of healthy eating and lifestyles practices. However, Individual needs and circumstances may vary so it's recommended to consult with a qualified healthcare professional or a registered dietician before making any significant changes to your diet or lifestyle.

The author and publisher of this book make no representations or warranties regarding the accuracy, completeness or applicability of the information contained herein. They also disclaim any liability for any damages or adverse effects resulting from the use or application of the information provided in this book. Every effort has been made to ensure that the information provided in this book is accurate and up to date at the time of publication. However, the author and publisher do not assume any responsibility for any errors or omissions that may occur.

It is important to remember that readers are solely responsible for their own health and wellbeing and any actions they take based on the information provided in this book are done of their own risk. It's best to consult with a qualified professional for personalized advice related to your specific dieting and health needs.

Dear Valued Readers,

I'm reaching out to kindly ask for a moment of your time to share your thoughts and experiences with my work.

Your feedback is incredibly important to me. It not only helps me understand what resonates with you but also guides me in shaping future content that aligns with your interests and needs.

If you could take a few minutes to leave a review, I would be deeply grateful. Your insights are valuable and greatly appreciated.

And if you have any questions, kindly reach me on this email: kariebishop67@gmail.com

Looking forward to reading your reviews!

TABLE OF CONTENT

INTRODUCTION

Are you having trouble gaining weight and sick of worrying about how you look? If so, smoothies for weight gain could be the answer you've been looking for.

I can speak from experience when I say that these scrumptious and nutrient-rich beverages may assist you in achieving your weight gain objectives in a safe and long-lasting manner.

Imagine being eager to start your day with a wonderful smoothie that not only tastes fantastic but also gives your body the nutrition it needs to flourish when you get up in the morning. Imagine going about your everyday tasks while feeling more energized, self-assured, and healthier.

That's precisely how I felt when I first learned about smoothies for weight gain. I had a hard time gaining weight and was sick of feeling unconfident and unwell. Yet, merely eating more wasn't sufficient. I wanted to increase my calorie and nutrient intake without becoming bloated or uncomfortable.

I then began experimenting with smoothies to help me gain weight. I soon realized that these beverages weren't only tasty and simple to create; they were also brimming with protein, good fats, and complex carbs that might support healthy muscle growth and weight gain.

Yet, not every smoothie is made equal. That is why I created this book of scrumptious and nutritious weight-gain smoothie recipes. Each recipe includes a selection of fruits and vegetables as well as protein-rich ingredients

13

including protein powder, Greek yogurt, and nut butter. Also, we'll demonstrate how to include wholesome fats in your smoothies, such as avocado, chia seeds, and coconut oil.

Together with the recipes, I'll also give you my best advice for using smoothies to gain the most weight. I'll demonstrate how to include smoothies into a balanced diet, how to add additional calories with healthy ingredients, and how to monitor your progress and modify your recipes as necessary.

I've seen fantastic results since including weight gain smoothies into my diet. I now have more muscle, more vitality, and a better sense of self-worth in my own body. And now, I want to use the power of weight-gain smoothies to assist you in achieving your weight-gain objectives and improving your health.

So, weight gain smoothies may help you achieve your objectives whether you're an athlete seeking to add muscle or simply someone who wants to feel more confident and healthier. Together, let's start along this path to your desired healthy weight.

SMOOTHIES' BENEFITS FOR WEIGHT GAIN

Smoothies provide an easy and delectable method to ingest additional calories and nutrients, making them a wonderful tool for people trying to gain weight.

<u>These are a few advantages of smoothies for gaining weight:</u>

1.**Simple-to-eat:** Smoothies provide a simple and practical approach to quickly ingesting a large number of calories and nutrients. This may be particularly beneficial for those who have a hectic schedule or have trouble eating enough calories throughout the day.

2.**Customizable**: Smoothies are simple to tailor to your dietary requirements and tastes, which may help guarantee that you are consuming the proper ratio of macronutrients (carbohydrates, protein, and fats) to promote weight growth. For instance, you may boost the amount of protein by adding more protein powder or nut butter, or you can increase the number of calories by adding additional healthy fats like avocado or coconut oil.

3.**Contains nutrients**: Smoothies may include a wide range of nutrients, including fruits, vegetables, nuts, and seeds. This may provide a selection of necessary vitamins and minerals that promote overall health and well-being. Superfoods with established health benefits like acai berries, spirulina, or maca powder are also included in many smoothie recipes.

4.**Smoothies are an excellent pre-workout or lunchtime snack** since they may provide you with a rapid surge of energy. Supplying more fuel for exercise may also assist objectives for weight gain.

5. **Digestive health:** By combining fiber-rich foods like leafy greens and chia seeds, smoothies may boost digestive health. This may encourage regularity

and enhance intestinal health in general.

6.**Variety:** You may experience a new taste combination every day with the wide variety of smoothie recipes and variants available. This might lessen boredom and make it simpler to follow a diet plan for weight growth.

7.Creating your smoothies at home might be far less expensive than purchasing pre-made meal replacement drinks or vitamins for weight gain. Also, the quality of the components you use is more under your control.

CHAPTER 1

What are Macronutrients?

The body needs a lot of macronutrients to produce energy, develop and repair tissues, and promote general health and well-being.
The three main macronutrients are **fat, protein, and carbs.**

1.Carbohydrates: The body's main source of energy is carbohydrate-based. These are converted into glucose, which the body uses as fuel. Carbohydrates come in two varieties: simple and complicated.
Simple carbs are included in processed meals, sweets, and fruits, and they easily break down into glucose. Complex carbs, which take longer to break down and are included in meals like whole grains, fruits, and vegetables, provide you with prolonged energy.

2.Protein: The formation and repair of biological tissues, such as muscle, bone, skin, and hair, depends on protein. In addition, it contributes to the synthesis of substances such as hormones and enzymes. Nine necessary amino acids—which the body cannot manufacture on its own and must get from dietary sources— makeup protein. Meat, fish, eggs, dairy products, legumes, and nuts are all excellent sources of protein.

3.Fat: Fat is crucial for the body's generation of hormones and other substances as well as for the storage of energy and insulation. Saturated and unsaturated fats are two different kinds. Animal goods like meat and dairy, as well as processed meals, contain saturated fats that should be taken in moderation. Unsaturated fats are crucial for heart health and may be found in foods like nuts, seeds, avocados, and fatty seafood.

To maintain general health and well-being, it's crucial to take a range of micronutrients, such as vitamins and minerals, in addition to these macronutrients.

Protein, carbs, and fats' effects on weight gain

The body depends on protein, carbs, and fats to get the vital elements it needs to develop and operate effectively, thus they all play a significant part in weight growth.

Detailed analysis of how each macronutrient contributes to weight gain

1.Protein: A crucial macronutrient for developing and rebuilding muscular tissue, protein is a need. You are destroying muscle tissue whenever you exercise or conduct strength training. A sufficient protein diet may assist muscle development and repair, which might result in weight gain. Moreover, protein is a satiating macronutrient, which means it may promote healthy weight gain by keeping you feeling full and content after meals and reducing overeating. Meat, fish, eggs, dairy products, legumes, and nuts are all excellent sources of protein.

2.Carbohydrates: As they are the body's main energy source, carbohydrates are a crucial macronutrient for promoting exercise and weight growth. Whole grains, fruits, and vegetables are examples of complex carbs that help maintain energy levels throughout the day and encourage physical activity.

Also, by giving the body the energy it needs for exercise, eating enough carbs may help prevent muscle loss and encourage muscular development.

3.Fats: Fats are an important macronutrient that is required for the generation of hormones, proper functioning of cells, and insulation. By giving the body a source of long-lasting energy, eating enough healthy fats may also aid in the promotion of healthy weight growth. Avocados, nuts, seeds, and fatty fish are good sources of good fats.

How to balance your smoothies' macronutrients

Achieving your weight gain objectives requires balancing the macronutrients in your smoothies.

The following advice will help you balance the macronutrients in your smoothies:

1.Start with a source of protein: Include a source of protein in your smoothies to help muscle development and repair. Greek yogurt, milk, nut butter, and protein powder are all excellent sources of protein for smoothies. Include 15 to 20 grams of protein minimum into your smoothie.

2. Including complex carbs in your smoothies may provide you with enduring energy all day long and encourage physical activity. Excellent sources of complex carbs for smoothies include oats, quinoa, fruit, and veggies. Your smoothie should have 30–40 grams of complex carbs.

3.Include healthy fats: Good fats may aid in the promotion of satiety, assist the creation of hormones, and serve as a source of long-lasting energy. Nuts, seeds, avocado, and coconut oil are excellent sources of healthful fats for smoothies. Include 10 to 15 grams of good fats in your smoothie.

4.Think about micronutrients: It's crucial to take into account the micronutrients in your smoothies in addition to the macronutrients. Vitamins and minerals are micronutrients that are crucial for general health and may help people gain weight. Leafy greens, and berries, as well as other fruits and vegetables, are excellent providers of vitamins for smoothies.

5.Ratios may be changed to suit your needs: Your particular requirements and objectives will determine the optimum macronutrient ratio for your smoothie.

You may need to consume more protein and carbohydrates while eating less fat if you want to gain weight. You may assist your weight gain objectives by working with a trained dietitian to make sure you are getting the proper macronutrient balance in your diet.

Tips for keeping track of your nutritional intake

Here are some guidelines for monitoring your nutritional intake:

1.Implement a food monitoring app: Apps that track your food consumption might be helpful tools for monitoring your nutritional intake. They provide you with information on the macronutrient and micronutrient composition of your food and let you record your meals and snacks. MyFitnessPal, Lose It!, and Cronometer is a few of the well-known food-tracking applications.

2.Maintain a food diary: Keeping a food journal might be a useful tool if you prefer to manually monitor your nutritional consumption. Record the macronutrient and micronutrient composition of everything you eat and drink throughout the day, including portion amounts. This might show you areas where your nutritional intake may need to be changed.

3.Employ measuring equipment: You can precisely measure your nutritional intake by using measuring instruments like measuring cups and food scales. Make sure you are getting the right amount of macronutrients and micronutrients by measuring out your servings and using these tools.

4.Study the nutrition facts on food labels to learn more about the macro- and micronutrient composition of packaged foods. Read the labels of the foods you buy to be sure you're choosing ones that will help you reach your nutritional consumption targets.

5.Meal preparation in advance may help you make sure you are getting the right balance of macronutrients and micronutrients in your diet. Plan your meals for the next week using a meal planning template, and be sure to include a range of nutrient-rich foods.

6.Get advice from a trained dietitian: A trained dietician might be a useful resource if you're having problems keeping track of your nutritional consumption or need assistance developing a nutrient-dense meal plan. You may get advice from a nutritionist on how to choose nutrient-rich foods and how to include them in your diet.

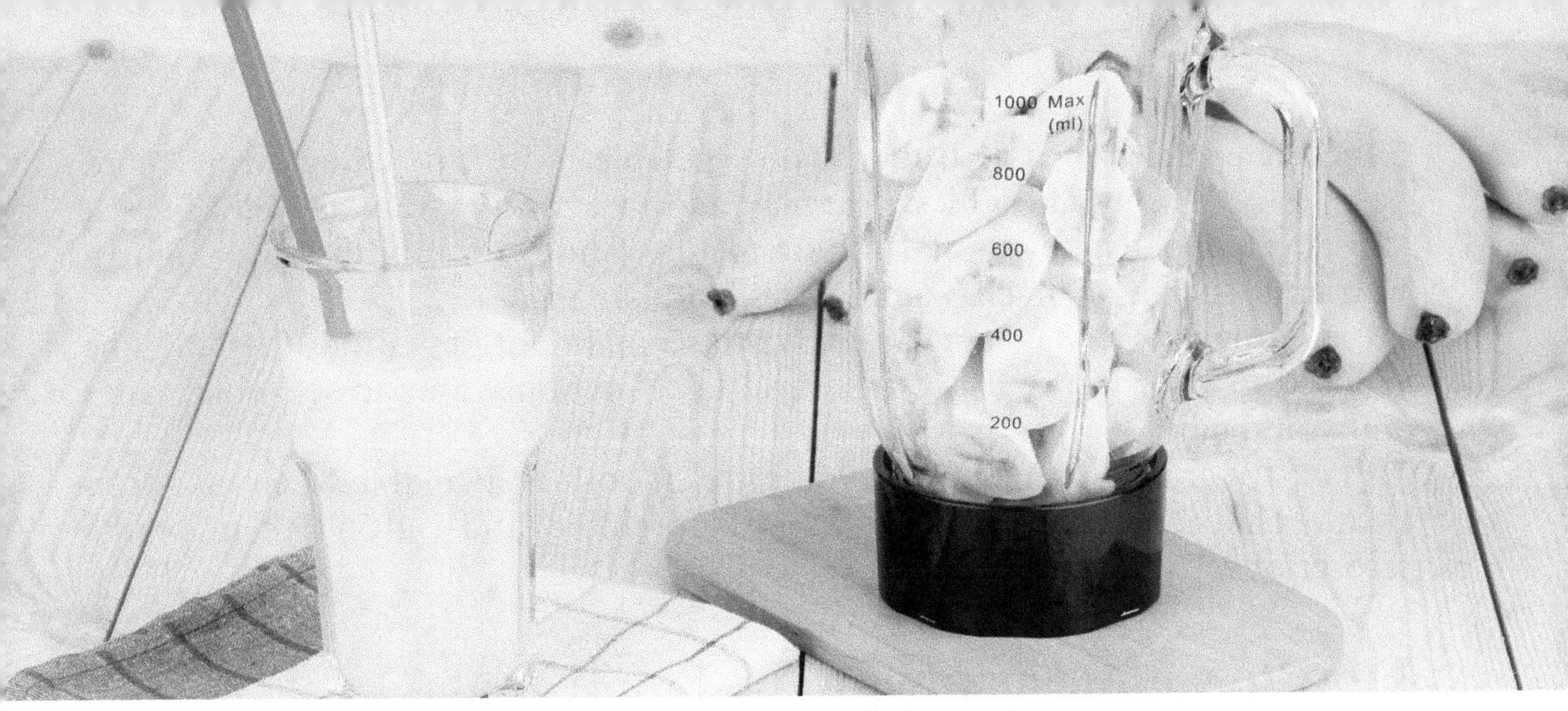

CHAPTER 2

How to Start Your Smoothie Weight Gain Journey

To guarantee that you are setting yourself up for success, there are a few crucial things to take before beginning a smoothie weight-gain program.

<u>Tips to help you start your smoothie weight gain journey:</u>

1.Establish your calorie requirements: Before you start using smoothies in your diet to encourage weight growth, it's essential to establish how many calories you need to eat daily to do so. A certified dietician or a calorie calculator may be used to determine this.

2.Establish a target for weight gain: Setting a weight gain target is crucial after you are aware of how many calories you must eat daily. You may monitor your development and maintain motivation by doing this. Aiming for a gain of 1-2 pounds every week is a reasonable target.

3.Choose a protein powder: Protein powder is a crucial component in smoothies for weight gain since it encourages muscle development and repair. Ideally, your protein powder should include at least 20 grams of protein per serving and be of good quality.

4.Choose wholesome fats: Smoothies for weight gain often include healthy fats like avocado, nut butter, and coconut oil as major sources of calories. To maintain general health, it's crucial to choose good fats.

5.Include nutrient-dense fruits and vegetables: By including fruits and vegetables in your smoothies, you may add taste and texture as well as assist satisfy your daily nutritional requirements. Choose foods that are high in nutrients, such as spinach, kale, berries, and bananas.

6.Play around with flavours: One advantage of smoothies is that they may be tailored to your tastes. Try out several taste combinations to see which ones suit you the best.

7.Plan: It's crucial to make sure you have smoothies available when you need them. Think about preparing things beforehand and putting them in the freezer or refrigerator.

How to set reasonable weight gain goals

Establishing reasonable weight gain goals is crucial to achieving your ideal weight in a healthy and long-lasting manner.

<u>Here are some guidelines for establishing reasonable weight-gain objectives:</u>

1.Determine your present body mass index (BMI): Based on your height and weight, your BMI calculates your body fat percentage. Determine if you are underweight, normal weight, overweight, or obese with its assistance. With an online calculator, you can quickly determine your BMI.

2.Choose a weight range that fits you best: A healthy weight range for your height and body type is your optimum weight range. To identify your optimal weight range, it's crucial to speak with a healthcare expert, such as a certified dietitian or doctor.

3.Establish a realistic target for weight gain: You may establish a reasonable weight increase target after determining your optimal weight range. It is advised to strive for a weekly weight increase of 0.5–1 pound. Depending on your beginning weight and general health, this may change.

4.Divide your objective into more manageable milestones: Establishing minor goals may keep you motivated and allow you to monitor your development. If your ultimate objective is to gain 10 pounds, for instance, you can set a milestone of gaining 2 pounds in the first month.

5.Evaluate your routine and lifestyle: It's crucial to take your way of life and regular routines into account when determining your weight gain objectives. It could be harder to gain weight, for instance, if you don't have access to many healthy food alternatives or have a hectic schedule. Setting smaller, more manageable objectives in this situation could be beneficial.

6.Track your progress: Monitoring your development might help you maintain motivation and make necessary corrections. You may track your development by weighing yourself often and maintaining a meal journal.

Tips for including smoothies in your diet

1.Using a quality blender. First Smooth and creamy smoothie must be made using a high-quality blender. To make blending simpler, look for a blender with a strong motor and a high capacity.

2.Choose the proper ingredients: Choose ingredients that are rich in calories and nutrients to make a smoothie that will help you gain weight. Fruits and vegetables like spinach and kale, nuts and seeds like almonds and chia seeds, healthy fats like avocado and coconut oil, and meals high in protein like Greek yogurt and protein powder may all fit into this category.

3.Try out a variety of flavors: Smoothies are a delicious way to try out new tastes and ingredients. To discover a taste, you like, try experimenting with various fruit, vegetable, and spice combinations.

4.Prepare a batch of smoothies in advance and store them in the fridge or freezer to save time during the week. This makes it simple to grab a smoothie while on the run or to quickly substitute a meal.

5.As a meal substitute, smoothies may be used: Some who find it difficult to prepare and consume a full meal may discover that smoothies are a fantastic meal replacement choice. Smoothies may be made more satisfying by adding protein powder and good fats, which can help you feel full until your next meal.

6.Make smoothies a regular part of your diet: Consider incorporating smoothies into your daily routine by consuming them as a post-workout recovery beverage or as a lunchtime snack.

7.Adapt to your dietary requirements: You may alter smoothies to suit your nutritional requirements and tastes. Use plant-based protein powder and dairy-free milk substitutes, for instance, if you're vegan.

8. Don't only depend on smoothies to get your nutrition: Although smoothies may be a fantastic tool for achieving weight gain objectives, it's crucial to keep in mind that they shouldn't be your only source of food.

To make sure you are receiving a balanced intake of nutrients, be sure to include a variety of whole foods in your diet.

How to design a smoothie weight-gain strategy that is effective for you

<u>Here are some guidelines for making a strategy that is effective for you:</u>

1.Identify your caloric requirements: Finding out how many calories you must consume daily to reach your weight gain objectives is the first step in developing a smoothie weight gain strategy. To calculate how many calories, you need each day, use a calorie calculator or speak with a trained nutritionist.

2.Choose foods that are high in nutrients: It's crucial to pick components for smoothies that are rich in nutrients and encourage weight growth. Fruits, vegetables, whole grains, good fats, and protein sources are included in this. Ingredients that are high in nutrients include things like bananas, avocados, oats, almonds, and protein powder.

3.Macronutrient balance: Each smoothie should have a combination of carbs, protein, and healthy fats to promote weight growth. Strive for a balance of around 40% carbs, 30% protein, and 30% good fats.

4.Schedule your meals: Making a schedule for your meals and snacks will help you stay on track with your daily caloric intake and a healthy diet. Also, it might assist you to avoid reaching for bad snacks or unhealthy foods when you're hungry.

5.Try new smoothie recipes to keep things interesting and to discover tastes and ingredients you like. Experiment with different recipes. Try diverse combinations of fruits, veggies, and other components without fear of failure.

6.Consistency is key: To achieve your weight gain objectives, consistency is essential. Strive to follow your smoothie weight-gain plan as closely as you can, and change it as necessary in light of your success and any advice from a healthcare provider.

CHAPTER 3

Selecting Healthy Ingredients for Smoothies to Gain Weight

<u>Here are some pointers for selecting nutritious components for smoothies that promote weight gain:</u>

1.Start with a base. You may use milk, yogurt, or a milk substitute like almond or soy milk as the foundation of your smoothie. These bases will give your smoothie a creamy texture and increase its protein and calorie content.

2.Fruits: Due to their high vitamin, mineral, and antioxidant content, fruits are a fantastic addition to any smoothie. But it's crucial to choose fruits with plenty of calories, such as bananas, mangos, and avocados. Also, these fruits include a lot of good fats, which are crucial for weight building.

3.Vegetables: Smoothies' nutritional density may be increased by including veggies without adding a lot of calories. Leafy greens are a great option since they are packed with vitamins and minerals, such as spinach and kale. Carrots and sweet potatoes are examples of sweet veggies that may naturally sweeten your smoothie.

4.Protein: Building and rebuilding muscle tissue, which is essential for weight growth, requires. Greek yogurt, nut butters, protein powders, and silken tofu are all excellent sources of protein for smoothies

5.Healthy Fats: By including healthy fats in your smoothies, you can up the calorie count while still getting essential nutrients. Chia seeds, avocado, coconut oil, and nut butter are a few excellent sources of healthful fats.

6.Try different tastes: Don't be hesitant to experiment with different tastes and ingredient pairings in your smoothies. Combine various fruits, veggies, and tastes to create the ideal concoction for you.

7. Portion control: It's crucial to consider portion sizes and calorie counts when selecting components for your weight gain smoothies. Although eating too many calories might result in undesired weight gain, healthful components can also deliver vital nutrients.

To ensure that you are healthily achieving your weight gain objectives, aim to incorporate a mix of macronutrients (protein, carbs, and fats) in your smoothies. You should also think about measuring your calorie consumption.

Ingredients high in calories for weight gain

You may add the following high-calorie components to your smoothies:

1.Nut butters: All three nut butters—almond, cashew, and peanut—are heavy in calories and have good fats. They may provide your smoothies with a rich, creamy texture as well as an increase in protein and good fats.

2.Avocado: Avocado is a fantastic source of good fats and may give your smoothies a creamy feel. Moreover, it is a good source of fiber, potassium, and vitamins C, K, and B6.

3.Greek yogurt: Greek yogurt has a lot of protein and gives smoothies a creamy texture. Calcium and vitamin D are also abundant in them.

4.Oats: Oats are a fantastic source of fiber and complex carbs. They may give your smoothies a substantial texture and make you feel fuller for longer.

5.Coconut milk has a lot of calories and good fats. It may give your smoothies a creamy texture and a tropical taste.

6.Dates: Rich in calories and fiber, dates are a natural sweetener. They may give your smoothies a delicious taste without using added sweets.

7.Hemp seeds include a lot of protein and good lipids. They may give your smoothies a nutty taste and an increase in omega-3 fatty acids.

When making smoothies with high-calorie components, it's crucial to pay attention to serving amounts and avoid going overboard. To make sure you are receiving a balanced and nutritious meal, it is also crucial to balance your smoothies with nutrient-dense items like fruits and vegetables.

Ingredients high in protein for muscle building

Protein is a necessary nutrient that is important for the growth and repair of muscular tissue. Protein-rich components should be included in smoothies if you want to gain weight and develop muscle.

<u>These are some high-protein foods to take into account:</u>

1.Greek yogurt: With an average of 17 grams of protein per 6-ounce serving, Greek yogurt is a fantastic source of protein. Probiotics in it may also help with intestinal health.

2.Whey protein powder is a quick-digesting protein that the body can easily absorb, making it the perfect post-workout supplement. Also, it contains a lot of important amino acids, which are necessary for both muscle development and repair.

3.Hemp Seeds: Hemp seeds contain all nine of the necessary amino acids, making them a complete protein source. They are a healthful addition to any smoothie since they are also high in fiber and good fats.

4.Chia Seeds: Chia seeds are a second supply of complete protein, high in fiber, and a good source of omega-3 fatty acids. They are a great addition to weight gain smoothies since they may help you feel content and full for extended periods.

5.Nut butters are a fantastic source of protein, good fats, and fiber. Examples include almonds and peanut butter. They may help keep you full and give smoothies a creamy texture.

6.Silken Tofu: With an average of 10 grams of plant-based protein per half-cup serving, silken tofu is a fantastic source of this kind of protein. It is a fantastic component for smoothies that help you gain weight since it is low in calories and fat.

7.Milk: With an average of 8 grams of protein per cup, milk is a great source of both calcium and protein. Smoothies might benefit from having their taste and creaminess increased.

It's crucial to pay attention to portion proportions and daily caloric consumption when adding protein-rich components to smoothies. For the key amino acids your body needs for muscle building and repair, try to incorporate a range of protein sources in your smoothies.

Ingredients rich in nutrients that improve the overall health

Every healthy diet, even one designed to help you gain weight, must include nutrient-dense foods. These components are loaded with vitamins, minerals, antioxidants, and other healthy elements that help enhance energy levels, promote weight growth, and generally improve health.

You may make smoothies to help you gain weight by using the following nutrient-dense ingredients:

1.Greens, leafy: Vitamins A, C, K, and folate are abundant in leafy greens including spinach, kale, and collard greens. They also include a lot of fiber, which helps to maintain a healthy digestive system and keep you feeling full.

2.Fruits and vegetables: Fruits and vegetables, including blueberries, strawberries, and raspberries, are rich in antioxidants that may help prevent cellular damage and inflammation. Moreover, they are a wonderful source of fiber, vitamin C, and other necessary nutrients.

3.Avocado: Avocado is an excellent source of monounsaturated and polyunsaturated fats, which may improve heart health and provide you with long-lasting energy. Vitamins C, K, and B6 as well as fiber and potassium are all abundant in avocado.

4.Nuts and seeds are great sources of fiber, protein, and healthy fats. Some examples of nuts and seeds include almonds, walnuts, chia seeds, and flaxseeds. They also include nutrients that are crucial for general health, such as zinc, magnesium, and vitamin E.

5.Greek yogurt: Greek yogurt is a fantastic source of protein, which is necessary for repairing and constructing muscle. Moreover, it has advantageous probiotics that may promote digestive health.

6.Medium-chain triglycerides (MCTs), which may serve as a rapid source of energy, are among the beneficial fats found in abundance in coconut milk. Moreover, it has vitamins and minerals including magnesium and iron.

7.The sweet potato Complex carbs, like those in sweet potatoes, may provide you with long-lasting energy. Moreover, they include a lot of fiber, vitamins A and C, and other necessary elements.

Along with helping you achieve your weight gain objectives, including these nutrient-dense components to your weight gain smoothies may have several positive health effects. Try out several pairings and tastes to see which ones are best for you.

Customizable options to fit dietary preferences

Individual dietary preferences and limits should be taken into account while developing weight gain smoothies. Thankfully, many items may be altered to suit different diets.

Alternatives for vegetarians and vegans

For those who eat vegetarian or vegan meals, plant-based protein sources like tofu, nut butters, and pea protein powder may provide the essential amino acids for muscle growth. Smoothie bases may be made using non-dairy milk substitutes such as almond, soy, or oat milk.

Alternatives for Gluten-Free

You may get your carbs from gluten-free grains like quinoa or oats. For increased protein, gluten-free protein powders made from hemp or brown rice may be used.

Alternatives for the paleo and whole30

Diets include using coconut milk or almond milk as a basis, along with nuts, seeds, and nut butters for protein and good fats.

Low-Carb Alternatives

For those seeking a low-carb alternative, ingredients like avocado, coconut oil, and nut butters may provide healthy fats, while protein powder and spinach can offer proteins.

Since not all substances may be effective for every person, it's vital to pay attention to your body and, if required, seek the advice of a healthcare professional or qualified dietitian. A tasty and nourishing weight gain smoothie may be made with a little experimenting to accommodate unique dietary tastes and requirements.

SMOOTHIE RECIPES
FOR WEIGHT GAIN
31

Banana Peanut Butter Powerhouse Smoothie

Prep Time: 5 minutes   **Servings: 1**

Ingredients

- 2 ripe bananas
- 2 tablespoons peanut butter
- 1 cup whole milk
- 1/4 cup oats
- 1 tablespoon honey
- Ice (optional)

Preparation

1. Blend all ingredients until smooth.
2. Optional: Add a handful of ice for a chilled texture.
3. Serve and enjoy

Nutritional Info: Calories: 450 Protein: 12g Fat: 20g Carbohydrates: 55g Fiber: 6g

Blueberry Almond Burst Smoothie

Prep Time: 5 minutes   **Servings: 1**

Ingredients

- 1/2 cup blueberries
- 1/4 cup almonds
- ·1 cup Greek yogurt
- 1 tablespoon chia seeds
- 1 cup almond milk

Preparation

1. 1.Blend all ingredients until well combined.
2. Adjust thickness with more almond milk if needed.
3. Serve and enjoy

Nutritional Info: Calories: 380 Protein: 15g Fat: 18g Carbohydrates: 40g Fiber: 8g

Chocolate Avocado Dream Smoothie

Prep Time: 5 minutes   **Servings: 1**

Ingredients

- 1/2 avocado
- 2 tablespoons cocoa powder
- 1 cup whole milk
- 1/4 cup oats
- 1 tablespoon maple syrup

Preparation

1. Blend all ingredients until creamy.
2. Top with a sprinkle of oats before serving

Nutritional Info: Calories: 420 Protein: 10g Fat: 22g Carbohydrates: 50g Fiber: 7g

Vanilla Berry Blast Smoothie

Prep Time: 5 minutes   **Servings: 1**

Ingredients

- 1 teaspoon vanilla extract
- 1/2 cup mixed berries (strawberries, blueberries, raspberries)
- 1 tablespoon honey
- 1/4 cup oats
- 1 cup whole milk

Preparation

1. Blend all the ingredients until smooth.
2. Garnish with additional berries if desired

Nutritional Info: Calories: 350 Protein: 9g Fat: 10g Carbohydrates: 50g Fiber: 6g

Pineapple Coconut Smoothie

Prep Time: 5 minutes   **Servings: 1**

Ingredients

- 1 cup diced pineapple
- 1/2 cup shredded coconut
- 1 cup coconut milk
- 1/2 lime (juiced)
- 1 tablespoon agave syrup

Preparation

1. Blend all ingredients until smooth.
2. Squeeze in lime juice and mix well.

Nutritional Info: Calories: 380 Protein: 5g Fat: 20g Carbohydrates: 50g Fiber: 7g

Strawberry Banana Nut Smoothie

Prep Time: 5 minutes   **Servings: 1**

Ingredients

- 1 cup strawberries
- 1 banana
- 1/4 cup chopped walnuts
- 1 tablespoon honey
- Honey (optional)
- 1 cup whole milk

Preparation

1. Blend all ingredients until smooth.
2. Add a drizzle of honey on top (optional).

Nutritional info: Calories: 410 Protein: 11g Fat: 18g Carbohydrates: 55g Fiber: 6g

Cherry Almond Butter Elixir Smoothie

Prep Time: 5 minutes   **Servings: 1**

Ingredients

- 1/2 cup cherries (pitted)
- 2 tablespoons almond butter
- 1 cup Greek yogurt
- 1/4 cup oats
- 1 tablespoon honey

Preparation

1. Blend all ingredients until smooth and creamy.
2. Garnish with a few whole cherries.

Nutritional info: Calories: 360 Protein: 14g Fat: 15g Carbohydrates: 45g Fiber: 7g

Apple Cinnamon Roll Smoothie

Prep Time: 5 minutes   **Servings: 1**

Ingredients

- 1 apple (cored and sliced)
- 1/4 cup oats
- 1 cup whole milk
- 1/2 teaspoon ground cinnamon
- 1 tablespoon maple syrup

Preparation

1. Blend all ingredients until smooth.
2. Sprinkle extra cinnamon on top before serving.

Nutritional info: Calories: 330 Protein: 9g Fat: 10g Carbohydrates: 55g Fiber: 7g

Raspberry Coconut Cream Smoothie

Prep Time: 5 minutes   **Servings: 1**

Ingredients

- 1/2 cup raspberries
- 1/2 cup coconut milk
- 1/2 cup Greek yogurt
- 1/4 cup shredded coconut
- 1 tablespoon honey

Preparation

1. Blend all the ingredients until smooth.
2. Serve and enjoy.

Nutritional info: Calories: 340 Protein: 10g Fat: 15g Carbohydrates: 45g Fiber: 6g

Oatmeal Raisin Cookie Shake Smoothie

Prep Time: 5 minutes   **Servings: 1**

Ingredients

- ·1/2 cup rolled oats
- ·1/4 cup raisins
- ·1 cup whole milk
- ·1/2 teaspoon vanilla extract
- ·Cinnamon (optional)

Preparation

1. Blend all ingredients until smooth.
2. Sprinkle with a pinch of cinnamon (optional).

Nutritional info: Calories: 330 Protein: 9g Fat: 8g Carbohydrates: 55g Fiber: 6g

Avocado Kale Protein Punch Smoothie

Prep Time: 5 minutes   **Servings: 1**

Ingredients

- 1/2 avocado
- 1 cup kale (stems removed)
- 1/2 cup Greek yogurt
- 1 scoop chocolate protein powder
- 1 cup almond milk

Preparation

1. Blend all ingredients until smooth.
2. Add more almond milk if a thinner consistency is desired.

Nutritional info: Calories: 420 Protein: 25g Fat: 18g Carbohydrates: 45g Fiber: 9g

Quinoa Berry Bliss Bowl Smoothie

Prep Time: 5 minutes   **Servings: 1**

Ingredients

- 1/4 cup cooked quinoa
- 1/2 cup mixed berries (strawberries, blueberries, raspberries)
- 1 tablespoon almond butter
- 1 cup coconut water
- 1/2 cup Greek yogurt

Preparation

1. Blend all the ingredients until well smooth.
2. .Garnish with a sprinkle of chia seeds

Nutritional info: Calories: 380 Protein: 15g Fat: 12g Carbohydrates: 55g Fiber: 8g

Chickpea Spinach Smoothie

Prep Time: 5 minutes   **Servings: 1**

Ingredients

- 1/2 cup canned chickpeas (rinsed and drained)
- 1 cup fresh spinach
- 1/2 banana
- 1 cup oat milk
- 1 tablespoon almond butter

Preparation

1. Blend all the ingredients until smooth.
2. Add more oat milk if needed for desired consistency.

Nutritional info: Calories: 370 Protein: 15g Fat: 12g Carbohydrates: 50g Fiber: 10g

Sweet Potato and Almond Smoothie

Prep Time: 5 minutes   **Servings: 1**

Ingredients

- 1/2 cup cooked sweet potato
- 1/4 cup almonds
- 1 cup vanilla-flavored Greek yogurt
- 1 cup almond milk
- Honey
- 1 tablespoon honey

Preparation

1. Blend all ingredients until smooth.
2. Top with a drizzle of honey before serving

Nutritional info: Calories: 400 Protein: 18g Fat: 15g Carbohydrates: 50g Fiber: 7g

Mango Avocado Turmeric Boost Smoothie

Prep Time: 5 minutes | **Servings: 1**

Ingredients

- 1 cup diced mango
- 1/2 avocado
- 1 teaspoon turmeric powder
- 1 tablespoon chia seeds
- 1 cup coconut water

Preparation

1. Blend all ingredients until smooth.
2. Adjust thickness with more coconut water if needed.

Nutritional info: Calories: 350 Protein: 8g Fat: 18g Carbohydrates: 45g Fiber: 9g

Black Bean and Berry Fusion Smoothie

Prep Time: 5 minutes | **Servings: 1**

Ingredients

- 1/2 cup canned black beans (rinsed and drained)
- 1/2 cup mixed berries (strawberries, blueberries, raspberries)
- 1 tablespoon almond butter
- 1 cup almond milk
- 1/2 banana

Preparation

1. Blend all the ingredients until smooth.
2. Garnish with a few whole berries.

Nutritional info: Calories: 360 Protein: 14g Fat: 12g Carbohydrates: 50g Fiber: 10g

Pistachio Banana Cream Smoothie

Prep Time: 5 minutes   **Servings: 1**

Ingredients

- 1/4 cup pistachios
- 1 banana
- 1 cup vanilla-flavored Greek yogurt
- 1 cup oat milk
- 1 tablespoon honey

Preparation

1. Blend all the ingredients until smooth.
2. Garnish with crushed pistachios on top.

Nutritional info: Calories: 380 Protein: 12g Fat: 15g Carbohydrates: 55g Fiber: 6g

Lentil and Banana Smoothie

Prep Time: 5 minutes   **Servings: 1**

Ingredients

- ·1/2 cup cooked lentils
- ·1 banana
- ·1 tablespoon almond butter
- ·1 cup vanilla-flavored Greek yogurt
- ·1 cup oat milk

Preparation

1. Blend all the ingredients until smooth.
2. Adjust sweetness with more banana if needed.

Nutritional info: Calories: 370 Protein: 16g Fat: 14g Carbohydrates: 50g Fiber: 8g

Raspberry Almond Quinoa Smoothie

Prep Time: 5 minutes   **Servings: 1**

Ingredients

- 1/4 cup cooked quinoa
- 1/2 cup raspberries
- 1/4 cup almonds
- 1 tablespoon honey
- 1 cup vanilla-flavored Greek yogurt

Preparation

1. Blend all the ingredients until smooth
2. Top with additional raspberries.

Nutritional info: Calories: 390 Protein: 15g Fat: 15g Carbohydrates: 50g Fiber: 7g

Butternut Squash and Walnut Smoothie

Prep Time: 5 minutes   **Servings: 1**

Ingredients

- 1/2 cup cooked butternut squash
- 1/4 cup walnuts
- 1 cup vanilla-flavored Greek yogurt
- 1 tablespoon maple syrup
- ·1 cup almond milk

Preparation

1. Blend all the ingredients until smooth.
2. Drizzle extra maple syrup on top for sweetness.

Nutritional info: Calories: 380 Protein: 13g Fat: 15g Carbohydrates: 50g Fiber: 6g

Nutty Banana Bread Smoothie

Prep Time: 5 minutes   **Servings: 1**

Ingredients

- 1 ripe banana
- 1/4 cup rolled oats
- 1 tablespoon almond butter
- 1 cup vanilla-flavored plant-based yogurt
- 1 cup almond milk
- 1/2 teaspoon cinnamon

Preparation

1. Blend all the ingredients until smooth.
2. Serve and enjoy.

Nutritional info: Calories: 380 Protein: 12g Fat: 15g Carbohydrates: 55g Fiber: 8g

Green Protein Powerhouse Smoothie

Prep Time: 5 minutes   **Servings: 1**

Ingredients

- 1 cup fresh spinach
- ·1/2 avocado
- 1/2 cup silken tofu
- 1 cup coconut water
- Ice cubes (optional)
- 1 tablespoon chia seeds

Preparation

1. Blend all the ingredients until well smooth.
2. Add ice cubes if desired and blend again.

Nutritional info: Calories: 350 Protein: 15g Fat: 20g Carbohydrates: 30g Fiber: 9g

Berry Almond Bliss Smoothie

Prep Time: 5 minutes   **Servings: 1**

Ingredients

- 1 cup mixed berries (strawberries, blueberries, raspberries)
- 1/4 cup almonds
- 1 cup almond milk
- Ice cubes (optional)
- ·1 tablespoon almond butter

Preparation

1. Blend all the ingredients until smooth.
2. Add ice cubes if desired and blend again

Nutritional info: Calories: 380 Protein: 12g Fat: 18g Carbohydrates: 50g Fiber: 9g

Coconut Mango Avocado Smoothie

Prep Time: 5 minutes   **Servings: 1**

Ingredients

- 1/2 cup diced mango
- 1/2 avocado
- 1/4 cup shredded coconut
- 1 cup coconut milk
- Ice cubes (optional)
- 1 tablespoon chia seeds

Preparation

1. Blend all the ingredients until smooth.
2. Add ice cubes if desired and blend again.

Nutritional info: Calories: 350 Protein: 8g Fat: 18g Carbohydrates: 45g Fiber: 9g

Pumpkin Spice Protein Elixir Smoothie

Prep Time: 5 minutes   **Servings: 1**

Ingredients

- 1/2 cup canned pumpkin puree
- 1/4 cup oats
- 1 scoop plant-based vanilla protein powder
- 1 cup almond milk
- Ice cubes (optional)
- 1 tablespoon maple syrup

Preparation

1. Blend all the ingredients until smooth.
2. Add ice cubes if desired and blend again

Nutritional info: Calories: 380 Protein: 20g Fat: 12g Carbohydrates: 55g Fiber: 8g

Vanilla Berry Protein Booster Smoothie

Prep Time: 5 minutes   **Servings: 1**

Ingredients

- 1 cup mixed berries (strawberries, blueberries, raspberries)
- 1 scoop vanilla plant-based protein powder
- 1 cup almond milk
- Ice cubes (optional)
- 1 tablespoon almond butter
- 1/2 banana

Preparation

1. Blend all the ingredients until smooth.
2. Add ice cubes if desired and blend again.

Nutritional info: Calories: 350 Protein: 18g Fat: 15g Carbohydrates: 45g Fiber: 9g

Spinach Avocado Citrus Smoothie

Prep Time: 5 minutes   **Servings: 1**

Ingredients

- 1 cup fresh spinach
- 1/2 avocado
- Juice of 1 orange
- 1 cup coconut water
- Ice cubes (optional)
- 1 tablespoon chia seeds
- 1/2 banana

Preparation

1. Blend all the ingredients until smooth.
2. Add ice cubes if desired and blend again.

Nutritional info: Calories: 320 Protein: 8g Fat: 15g Carbohydrates: 45g Fiber: 10g

Blueberry Almond Kale Twist Smoothie

Prep Time: 5 minutes   **Servings: 1**

Ingredients

- 1/2 cup blueberries
- 1/4 cup almonds
- 1 cup kale (stems removed)
- 1 cup almond milk
- Ice cubes (optional)
- 1 tablespoon almond butter
- 1/2 banana

Preparation

1. .Blend all the ingredients until smooth.
2. Add ice cubes if desired and blend again.

Nutritional info: Calories: 350 Protein: 12g Fat: 18g Carbohydrates: 45g Fiber: 9g

Mango Coconut Protein Smoothie

Prep Time: 5 minutes | **Servings: 1**

Ingredients

- 1 cup diced mango
- 1/4 cup shredded coconut
- 1 scoop plant-based protein powder
- 1 cup coconut milk
- Ice cubes (optional)
- 1 tablespoon chia seeds

Preparation

1. Blend all the ingredients until smooth.
2. Add ice cubes if desired and blend again.

Nutritional info: Calories: 370 Protein: 20g Fat: 15g Carbohydrates: 45g Fiber: 8g

Raspberry Pistachio Smoothie

Prep Time: 5 minutes | **Servings: 1**

Ingredients

- 1/2 cup raspberries
- 1/4 cup pistachios
- 1/2 banana
- 1 cup almond milk
- Ice cubes (optional)
- 1 tablespoon almond butter

Preparation

1. Blend all the ingredients until smooth.
2. Add ice cubes if desired and blend again.

Nutritional info: Calories: 360 Protein: 10g Fat: 18g Carbohydrates: 45g Fiber: 8g

Tropical Macadamia Smoothie

Prep Time: 5 minutes   **Servings: 1**

Ingredients

- 1 cup diced pineapple
- 1/2 cup full-fat coconut milk
- 1/4 cup macadamia nuts
- 1 cup coconut water
- Ice cubes (optional)
- 1 tablespoon honey
- 1 banana

Preparation

1. Blend all the ingredients until smooth.
2. Add ice cubes if desired and blend again.

Nutritional info: Calories: 520 Protein: 5g Fat: 35g Carbohydrates: 55g Fiber: 6g

Blueberry Almond Smoothie

Prep Time: 5 minutes   **Servings: 1**

Ingredients

- 1 cup blueberries
- 1/4 cup almonds
- 1/2 cup full-fat coconut milk
- 1 tablespoon maple syrup
- Ice cubes (optional)
- 1 cup almond milk
- 1 tablespoon almond butter

Preparation

1. Blend all the ingredients until smooth.
2. Add ice cubes if desired and blend again.

Nutritional info: Calories: 550 Protein: 10g Fat: 40g Carbohydrates: 45g Fiber: 8g

Caramel Pecan Smoothie

Prep Time: 5 minutes   **Servings: 1**

Ingredients

- 2 tablespoons pecans
- 1 banana
- 1/4 cup oats
- 1 tablespoon honey
- Ice cubes (optional)
- 1 cup whole milk
- 1 tablespoon caramel syrup

Preparation

1. Blend all the ingredients until smooth.
2. Add ice cubes if desired and blend again.

Nutritional info: Calories: 580 Protein: 12g Fat: 28g Carbohydrates: 70g Fiber: 7g

Mango Pistachio Smoothie

Prep Time: 5 minutes   **Servings: 1**

Ingredients

- 1 cup diced mango
- 1/4 cup pistachios
- 1/2 avocado
- 1 cup coconut milk
- Ice cubes (optional)
- 1 tablespoon honey

Preparation

1. Blend all the ingredients until smooth.
2. Add ice cubes if desired and blend again.

Nutritional info: Calories: 510 Protein: 8g Fat: 35g Carbohydrates: 50g Fiber: 7g

Peanut Butter Banana Nut Smoothie

Prep Time: 5 minutes   **Servings: 1**

Ingredients

- 2 tablespoons peanut butter
- 1 banana]
- 1/4 cup walnuts
- 1 tablespoon maple syrup
- Ice cubes (optional)
- 1 cup whole milk
- 1/4 cup granola

Preparation

1. Blend all the ingredients until smooth.
2. Add ice cubes if desired and blend again.

Nutritional info: Calories: 590 Protein: 15g Fat: 35g Carbohydrates: 60g Fiber: 7g

Vanilla Date Cinnamon Cream Smoothie

Prep Time: 5 minutes   **Servings: 1**

Ingredients

- 2 dates (pitted)
- 1 scoop vanilla protein powder
- 1/2 cup Greek yogurt
- 1 tablespoon honey
- Ice cubes (optional)
- 1/2 teaspoon cinnamon
- 1 cup whole milk

Preparation

1. Blend all the ingredients until smooth.
2. Add ice cubes if desired and blend again.

Nutritional info: Calories: 540 Protein: 22g Fat: 15g Carbohydrates: 70g Fiber: 6g

Banana Walnut Butterscotch Smoothie

Prep Time: 5 minutes　　　**Servings: 1**

Ingredients

- 2 bananas
- 1/4 cup walnuts
- 1 tablespoon butterscotch syrup
- 1 tablespoon honey
- Ice cubes (optional)
- 1 cup whole milk

Nutritional info: Calories: 550 Protein: 10g Fat: 30g Carbohydrates: 65g Fiber: 6g

Preparation

1. Blend all the ingredients until smooth.
2. Add ice cubes if desired and blend again.

Raspberry Coconut Cashew Smoothie

Prep Time: 5 minutes　　　**Servings: 1**

Ingredients

- 1/2 cup raspberries
- 1/4 cup cashews
- 1/2 cup full-fat coconut milk
- 1 tablespoon agave syrup
- Ice cubes (optional)
- 1 cup almond milk
- 1 tablespoon coconut oil

Nutritional info: Calories: 530 Protein: 8g Fat: 35g Carbohydrates: 50g Fiber: 7g

Preparation

1. Blend all the ingredients until smooth.
2. Add ice cubes if desired and blend again.

Cherry Almond Chocolate Smoothie

Prep Time: 5 minutes **Servings: 1**

Ingredients

- 1/2 cup cherries (pitted)
- 1/4 cup almonds
- 1 tablespoon cacao powder
- 1 tablespoon honey
- Ice cubes (optional)
- 1 cup whole milk

Preparation

1. Blend all the ingredients until smooth.
2. Add ice cubes if desired and blend again.

Nutritional info: Calories: 560 Protein: 12g Fat: 30g Carbohydrates: 65g Fiber: 8g

Fig Pistachio Cream Dream Smoothie

Prep Time: 5 minutes **Servings: 1**

Ingredients

- 2 dried figs
- 1/4 cup shelled pistachios
- 1/2 cup Greek yogurt
- 1 tablespoon honey
- Ice cubes (optional)
- 1 cup whole milk

Preparation

1. Blend all the ingredient until smooth.
2. Add ice cubes if desired and blend again.

Nutritional info: Calories: 540 Protein: 14g Fat: 28g Carbohydrates: 60g Fiber: 6g

Banana Protein Power House Smoothie

Prep Time: 5 minutes   **Servings: 1**

Ingredients

- 2 ripe bananas
- 1/4 cup almonds
- 1 scoop vanilla protein powder
- 1 cup Greek yogurt
- 1 cup almond milk
- 1 tablespoon honey
- Ice cubes (optional)

Preparation

1. Blend all the ingredients until smooth.
2. Serve and enjoy

Nutritional info: Calories: 480 Protein: 25g Fat: 18g Carbohydrates: 55g Fiber: 8g

Berry Quinoa Protein Boost Smoothie

Prep Time: 5 minutes   **Servings: 1**

Ingredients

- 1/2 cup mixed berries (strawberries, blueberries, raspberries)
- 1/4 cup cooked quinoa
- 1 scoop plant-based protein powder
- 1 cup Greek yogurt
- 1 cup coconut water
- 1 tablespoon maple syrup
- Ice cubes (optional)

Preparation

1. Blend all the ingredients together until smooth
2. Serve and enjoy

Nutritional info: Calories: 460 Protein: 22g Fat: 12g Carbohydrates: 60g Fiber: 9g

Chocolate Avocado Hemp Elixir Smoothie

Prep Time: 5 minutes   **Servings: 1**

Ingredients

- 1/2 avocado
- 2 tablespoons hemp seeds
- 1 tablespoon cacao powder
- 1 scoop chocolate protein powder
- 1 cup almond milk
- 1 tablespoon honey
- Ice cubes (optional)

Preparation

1. Blend all the ingredients until smooth.
2. Serve and enjoy

Nutritional info: Calories: 520 Protein: 20g Fat: 30g Carbohydrates: 40g Fiber: 9g

Pineapple Chia Protein Smoothie

Prep Time: 5 minutes   **Servings: 1**

Ingredients

- 1 cup diced pineapple
- 1 scoop vanilla protein powder
- 2 tablespoons chia seeds
- 1 cup Greek yogurt
- 1 cup coconut water
- 1 tablespoon agave syrup
- Ice cubes (optional)

Preparation

1. 1. Blend all the ingredients together until smooth
2. Serve and enjoy

Nutritional info: Calories: 480 Protein: 24g Fat: 15g Carbohydrates: 55g Fiber: 8g

Mango Lentil Protein Punch Smoothie

Prep Time: 5 minutes   Servings: 1

Ingredients

- 1 cup diced mango
- 1/4 cup cooked red lentils (cooled)
- 1 scoop plant-based protein powder
- 1 cup almond milk
- 1 tablespoon honey
- 1/2 teaspoon turmeric (optional)
- Ice cubes (optional)

Preparation

1. Blend all the ingredients until smooth.
2. Serve and enjoy

Nutritional info: Calories: 450 Protein: 22g Fat: 10g Carbohydrates: 60g Fiber: 8g

Strawberry Basil Protein Smoothie

Prep Time: 5 minutes   Servings: 1

Ingredients

- 1 cup strawberries
- 1/4 cup fresh basil leaves
- 1 scoop vanilla protein powder
- 1 cup Greek yogurt
- 1 cup coconut water
- 1 tablespoon honey
- Ice cubes (optional)

Preparation

1. 1. Blend all the ingredients together until smooth
2. Serve and enjoy

Nutritional info: Calories: 470 Protein: 23g Fat: 10g Carbohydrates: 60g Fiber: 7g

Kiwi Hemp Protein Smoothie

Prep Time: 5 minutes   **Servings: 1**

Ingredients

- 2 kiwis (peeled and sliced)
- 2 tablespoons hemp seeds
- 1 scoop chocolate protein powder
- 1 cup almond milk
- 1 tablespoon agave syrup
- Ice cubes (optional)

Nutritional info: Calories: 490 Protein: 21g Fat: 25g Carbohydrates: 50g Fiber: 8g

Preparation

1. Blend all the ingredients until smooth.
2. Serve and enjoy

Spinach Walnut Protein Green Goddess Smoothie

Prep Time: 5 minutes   **Servings: 1**

Ingredients

- 1 cup fresh spinach
- 1/4 cup walnuts
- 1 scoop vanilla protein powder
- 1 banana
- 1 cup almond milk
- 1 tablespoon honey
- Ice cubes (optional)

Nutritional info: Calories: 490 Protein: 22g Fat: 20g Carbohydrates: 60g Fiber: 9g

Preparation

1. Blend all the ingredients together until smooth
2. Serve and enjoy

Peach Cashew Protein Smoothie

Prep Time: 5 minutes   Servings: 1

Ingredients

- 1 cup diced peaches
- 1/4 cup cashews
- 1 scoop plant-based protein powder
- 1 cup Greek yogurt
- 1 cup coconut water
- 1 tablespoon maple syrup
- Ice cubes (optional)

Preparation

1. Blend all the ingredients until smooth.
2. Serve and enjoy

Nutritional info: Calories: 470 Protein: 24g Fat: 15g Carbohydrates: 55g Fiber: 7g

Blackberry Almond Protein Smoothie

Prep Time: 5 minutes   Servings: 1

Ingredients

- 1 cup blackberries
- 1/4 cup almonds
- 1 scoop vanilla protein powder
- 1 cup Greek yogurt
- 1 cup almond milk
- 1 tablespoon agave syrup
- Ice cubes (optional)

Preparation

1. Blend all the ingredients together until smooth
2. Serve and enjoy

Nutritional info: Calories: 490 Protein: 26g Fat: 20g Carbohydrates: 50g Fiber: 9g

WEIGHT GAIN PRE-WORKOUT SMOOTHIE RECIPES

Banana Berry Blast Smoothie

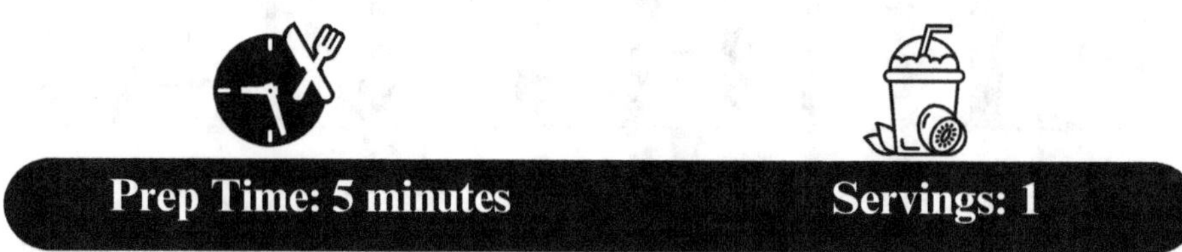

Prep Time: 5 minutes **Servings: 1**

Ingredients

- 1 banana
- 1/2 cup mixed berries (strawberries, blueberries, raspberries)
- 1 scoop vanilla protein powder
- 1/4 cup rolled oats
- 1 cup almond milk
- 1 tablespoon almond butter
- Ice cubes (optional)

Nutritional info: Calories: 420 Protein: 20g Fat: 15g Carbohydrates: 55g Fiber: 8g

Preparation

1. Blend all the ingredients until smooth.
2. Serve and enjoy

Pineapple Coconut Power Punch Smoothie

Prep Time: 5 minutes **Servings: 1**

Ingredients

- 1 cup diced pineapple
- 1/4 cup shredded coconut
- 1 scoop plant-based protein powder
- 1/2 cup Greek yogurt
- 1 cup coconut water
- 1 tablespoon honey
- Ice cubes (optional)

Nutritional info: Calories: 380 Protein: 18g Fat: 15g Carbohydrates: 50g Fiber: 7g

Preparation

1. Blend all the ingredients together until smooth
2. Serve and enjoy

Chocolate Coffee Kickstart Smoothie

Prep Time: 5 minutes **Servings: 1**

Ingredients

- 1 cup brewed coffee (cooled)
- 1 scoop chocolate protein powder
- 1/4 cup rolled oats
- 1 banana
- 1 tablespoon almond butter
- 1 cup almond milk
- Ice cubes (optional)

Nutritional info: Calories: 380 Protein: 22g Fat: 15g Carbohydrates: 45g Fiber: 8g

Preparation

1. Blend all the ingredients until smooth.
2. Serve and enjoy

Mango Basil Smoothie

Prep Time: 5 minutes **Servings: 1**

Ingredients

- 1 cup diced mango
- 1/4 cup fresh basil leaves
- 1 scoop vanilla protein powder
- 1/2 cup Greek yogurt
- 1 cup coconut water
- 1 tablespoon agave syrup
- Ice cubes (optional)

Nutritional info: Calories: 370 Protein: 20g Fat: 12g Carbohydrates: 50g Fiber: 7g

Preparation

1. Blend all the ingredients together until smooth
2. Serve and enjoy

Blueberry Mint Smoothie

Prep Time: 5 minutes   **Servings: 1**

Ingredients

- 1/2 cup blueberries
- 1/4 cup fresh mint leaves
- 1 scoop plant-based protein powder
- 1 cup almond milk
- 1 tablespoon chia seeds
- 1 tablespoon honey
- Ice cubes (optional)

Preparation

1. Blend all the ingredients until smooth.
2. Serve and enjoy

Nutritional info: Calories: 340 Protein: 16g Fat: 12g Carbohydrates: 45g Fiber: 8g

Raspberry Spinach Stamina Booster Smoothie

Prep Time: 5 minutes   **Servings: 1**

Ingredients

- 1/2 cup raspberries
- 1 cup fresh spinach
- ·1 scoop chocolate protein powder
- 1/2 cup Greek yogurt
- 1 cup almond milk
- 1 tablespoon almond butter
- Ice cubes (optional)

Preparation

1. Blend all the ingredients together until smooth
2. Serve and enjoy

Nutritional info: Calories: 370 Protein: 22g Fat: 15g Carbohydrates: 45g Fiber: 9g

Kiwi Coconut Citrus Smoothie

Prep Time: 5 minutes Servings: 1

Ingredients

- 2 kiwis (peeled and sliced)
- 1/4 cup shredded coconut
- 1 scoop vanilla protein powder
- 1 cup coconut water
- 1 tablespoon agave syrup
- Ice cubes (optional)

Preparation

1. Blend all the ingredients until smooth.
2. Serve and enjoy

Nutritional info: Calories: 360 Protein: 18g Fat: 12g Carbohydrates: 50g Fiber: 8g

Apple Cinnamon Energy Elixir Smoothie

Prep Time: 5 minutes Servings: 1

Ingredients

- 1 apple (cored and sliced)
- 1 scoop vanilla protein powder
- 1/4 cup almonds
- 1 cup almond milk
- 1 tablespoon maple syrup
- 1/2 teaspoon cinnamon
- ·Ice cubes (optional)

Preparation

1. Blend all the ingredients together until smooth
2. Serve and enjoy

Nutritional info: Calories: 390 Protein: 20g Fat: 15g Carbohydrates: 50g Fiber: 8g

Carrot Orange Protein Smoothie

Prep Time: 5 minutes　　　**Servings: 1**

Ingredients

- 1 cup carrots (peeled and sliced)
- 1/2 cup orange juice
- 1 scoop plant-based protein powder
- 1/4 cup cashews
- 1 cup coconut water
- 1 tablespoon honey
- Ice cubes (optional)

Nutritional info: Calories: 400 Protein: 19g Fat: 14g Carbohydrates: 55g Fiber: 7g

Preparation

1. Blend all the ingredients until smooth.
2. Serve and enjoy

Pomegranate Walnut Power Surge Smoothie

Prep Time: 5 minutes　　　**Servings: 1**

Ingredients

- 1/2 cup pomegranate seeds
- 1/4 cup walnuts
- 1 scoop chocolate protein powder
- 1 cup almond milk
- 1 tablespoon honey
- Ice cubes (optional)

Nutritional info: Calories: 410 Protein: 20g Fat: 15g Carbohydrates: 50g Fiber: 8g

Preparation

1. Blend all the ingredients together until smooth
2. Serve and enjoy

MUSCLE RECOVERY SMOOTHIES FOR POST-WORKOUT

Cherry Almond Protein Smoothie

Prep Time: 5 minutes   **Servings: 1**

Ingredients

- 1/2 cup cherries (pitted)
- 1/4 cup almonds
- 1 scoop vanilla protein powder
- 1 cup Greek yogurt
- 1 cup almond milk
- 1 tablespoon honey
- Ice cubes (optional)

Preparation

1. Blend all the ingredients until smooth.
2. Serve and enjoy

Nutritional info: Calories: 430 Protein: 24g Fat: 18g Carbohydrates: 50g Fiber: 7g

Mango Turmeric Recovery Blend

Prep Time: 5 minutes   **Servings: 1**

Ingredients

- 1 cup diced mango
- 1/2 teaspoon turmeric
- 1 scoop plant-based protein powder
- 1 cup coconut water
- ·1 tablespoon chia seeds
- 1 tablespoon agave syrup
- Ice cubes (optional)

Preparation

1. Blend all the ingredients together until smooth
2. Serve and enjoy

Nutritional info: Calories: 380 Protein: 20g Fat: 15g Carbohydrates: 45g Fiber: 8g

Spinach Pineapple Protein

Prep Time: 5 minutes   **Servings: 1**

Ingredients

- 1 cup fresh spinach
- 1 cup diced pineapple
- 1 scoop vanilla protein powder
- 1/2 avocado
- 1 cup coconut water
- 1 tablespoon honey
- Ice cubes (optional)

Preparation

1. Blend all the ingredients until smooth.
2. Serve and enjoy

Nutritional info: Calories: 410 Protein: 22g Fat: 18g Carbohydrates: 50g Fiber: 9g

Chocolate Peanut Butter Smoothie

Prep Time: 5 minutes   **Servings: 1**

Ingredients

- 1 scoop chocolate protein powder
- 2 tablespoons peanut butter
- 1 banana
- 1/4 cup oats
- 1 cup whole milk
- 1 tablespoon honey
- Ice cubes (optional)

Preparation

1. Blend all the ingredients together until smooth
2. Serve and enjoy

Nutritional info: Calories: 470 Protein: 25g Fat: 20g Carbohydrates: 55g Fiber: 7g

Blueberry Avocado Protein Smoothie

Prep Time: 5 minutes | **Servings: 1**

Ingredients

- 1/2 cup blueberries
- 1/2 avocado
- 1 scoop vanilla protein powder
- 1/4 cup almonds
- 1 cup almond milk
- 1 tablespoon agave syrup
- Ice cubes (optional)

Nutritional info: Calories: 450 Protein: 23g Fat: 20g Carbohydrates: 50g Fiber: 8g

Preparation

1. Blend all the ingredients until smooth.
2. Serve and enjoy

Pineapple Coconut Hydration Smoothie

Prep Time: 5 minutes | **Servings: 1**

Ingredients

- 1 cup diced pineapple
- 1/4 cup shredded coconut
- 1 scoop plant-based protein powder
- 1 cup coconut water
- 1 tablespoon chia seeds
- 1 tablespoon honey
- Ice cubes (optional)

Nutritional info: Calories: 380 Protein: 18g Fat: 15g Carbohydrates: 50g Fiber: 7g

Preparation

1. Blend all the ingredients together until smooth
2. Serve and enjoy

Raspberry Beetroot Recovery Smoothie

Prep Time: 5 minutes   **Servings: 1**

Ingredients

- 1/2 cup raspberries
- 1/2 cup cooked beetroot (cooled)
- 1 scoop chocolate protein powder
- 1/2 cup Greek yogurt
- 1 cup almond milk
- 1 tablespoon honey
- Ice cubes (optional)

Preparation

1. Blend all the ingredients until smooth.
2. Serve and enjoy

Nutritional info: Calories: 420 Protein: 22g Fat: 15g Carbohydrates: 55g Fiber: 9g

Green Tea Mango Protein Smoothie

Prep Time: 5 minutes   **Servings: 1**

Ingredients

- 1 cup brewed green tea (cooled)
- 1 cup diced mango
- 1 scoop vanilla protein powder
- 1/4 cup cashews
- 1 cup coconut water
- 1 tablespoon agave syrup
- ·Ice cubes (optional)

Preparation

1. Blend all the ingredients together until smooth
2. Serve and enjoy

Nutritional info: Calories: 410 Protein: 20g Fat: 15g Carbohydrates: 50g Fiber: 8g

Strawberry Basil Muscle Soother Smoothie

Prep Time: 5 minutes   Servings: 1

Ingredients

- 1/2 cup strawberries
- 1/4 cup fresh basil leaves
- 1 scoop plant-based protein powder
- 1/2 cup Greek yogurt
- 1 cup almond milk
- 1 tablespoon honey
- Ice cubes (optional)

Preparation

1. Blend all the ingredients until smooth.
2. Serve and enjoy

Nutritional info: Calories: 380 Protein: 19g Fat: 15g Carbohydrates: 50g Fiber: 7g

Peanut Butter Banana Muscle Builder Smoothie

Prep Time: 5 minutes   Servings: 1

Ingredients

- 2 bananas
- 2 tablespoons peanut butter
- 1 scoop chocolate protein powder
- 1/4 cup oats
- 1 cup whole milk
- 1 tablespoon honey
- Ice cubes (optional)

Preparation

1. Blend all the ingredients together until smooth
2. Serve and enjoy

Nutritional info: Calories: 480 Protein: 26g Fat: 20g Carbohydrates: 60g Fiber: 7g

CHAPTER 7

Smoothies as meal replacements for weight gain

Smoothies that double as meals may be a fantastic method to increase your calorie intake and help you gain weight, particularly if you struggle to consume enough food or have a low appetite.

It's crucial to eat more calories than you expend to acquire weight. You may do this with the aid of meal replacement smoothies, which provide a high-calorie, nutrient-dense meal in a handy and simple-to-digest format.

How to make meal replacement smoothies that can help you gain weight

1.Make use of calorie-dense ingredients: Choose ingredients with a lot of calories if you want your smoothie to have more calories. Nut butters, avocados, coconut oil, whole milk, yogurt, and protein powder are all excellent choices.

2.Add healthy fats: A diet for weight gain should include healthy fats since they are a concentrated source of calories and are necessary for hormone synthesis and cell expansion.

For smoothies, chia seeds, flaxseeds, hemp seeds, almonds, and nut butters are excellent sources of healthful fats.

3.Incorporate protein: Protein helps prevent muscle loss during weight gain and is essential for muscle development and repair. Greek yogurt, cottage cheese, tofu, nut butters, and protein powder are all excellent sources of protein for smoothies.

4.**When feasible, use whole foods over protein powders** since whole foods tend to have more nutrients. Protein powders may be a simple method to increase the protein content of your smoothie.

Using whole food sources of protein, such as Greek yogurt or cottage cheese, as well as fresh or frozen fruits and vegetables is necessary.

5.**Try out various flavors:** To keep your smoothies interesting and tasty, try out various flavor combinations. To produce a distinctive taste profile, you may combine different fruits, spices, and sweeteners.

Individual smoothie recipes that may be customized

Smoothies are a tasty and practical method to include a lot of nutrients in a single meal or snack. You may build a recipe that meets your specific requirements and preferences since they are so adaptable and flexible.

You may make a smoothie that is customized to your dietary requirements and tastes by following a basic recipe and experimenting with other components.

Breakdown of the components of a customizable smoothie recipe

1.**Water base:** Your smoothie's liquid base serves as itsframework and supplies the liquid needed to combine the other components.

The smoothie gains taste and nutrients as a result. Almond milk, coconut milk, ordinary milk, fruit juice, or water are just a few of the beverage options available. Also, you may mix other liquids to create a special taste.

2.**Fruits and veggies:** Increasing your daily dose of vitamins, minerals, and fiber is simple by adding fruits and vegetables to your smoothie. Fruits and vegetables may be used either fresh or frozen, depending on what is available and what you desire. Bananas, berries, spinach, kale, carrots, and avocados are a few healthy alternatives. Also, you may experiment with various pairings to develop distinctive tastes.

3.**Protein:** A smoothie's protein content is crucial for muscle development and repair as well as general wellness. Protein powder, Greek yogurt, nut butters, tofu, or even cooked chicken or beef are all excellent sources of protein. Choose a source of protein that complements your dietary requirements and tastes.

4.Omega-3 fatty acids and other essential nutrients may be found in healthy fats, which you can also add to your smoothie to help you feel content and full. Chia seeds, flax seeds, avocado, nut butter, and coconut oil are all recommended alternatives.

5.Sweeteners and flavourings: You may add sweeteners and flavourings to your smoothie to improve its taste. Honey, maple syrup, agave nectar, vanilla extract, cocoa powder, or cinnamon are a few flavourful alternatives.

Take care while adding sweeteners since certain varieties might be heavy in calories and sugar.

4-WEEK SMOOTHIE MEAL PLAN

How to prepare the smoothies are discussed in the book.

DAYS	BREAKFAST	LUNCH	DINNER
1	Banana Peanut Butter Powerhouse Smoothie	Quinoa Berry Bliss Bowl Smoothie	Mango Lentil Protein Punch Smoothie
2	Blueberry Almond Burst Smoothie	Chickpea Spinach Smoothie	Chocolate Avocado Dream Smoothie
3	Vanilla Berry Blast Smoothie	Raspberry Coconut Cashew Smoothie	Pistachio Banana Cream Smoothie
4	Pineapple Coconut Smoothie	Sweet Potato and Almond Smoothie	Black Bean and Berry Fusion Smoothie

DAYS	BREAKFAST	LUNCH	DINNER
5	Strawberry Banana Nut Smoothie	Mango Avocado Turmeric Boost Smoothie	Fig Pistachio Cream Dream Smoothie
6	Cherry Almond Butter Elixir Smoothie	Raspberry Almond Quinoa Smoothie	Blueberry Almond Kale Twist Smoothie
7	Apple Cinnamon Roll Smoothie	Nutty Banana Bread Smoothie	Vanilla Date Cinnamon Cream Smoothie
8	Peanut Butter Banana Nut Smoothie	Mango Pistachio Smoothie	Chocolate Avocado Hemp Elixir Smoothie
9	Banana Walnut Butterscotch Smoothie	Strawberry Basil Protein Smoothie	Pineapple Chia Protein Smoothie

DAYS	BREAKFAST	LUNCH	DINNER
10	Raspberry Pistachio Smoothie	Kiwi Hemp Protein Smoothie	Mango Coconut Protein Smoothie
11	Blueberry Almond Smoothie	Caramel Pecan Smoothie	Spinach Walnut Protein Green Goddess Smoothie
12	Berry Quinoa Protein Boost Smoothie	Chocolate Avocado Dream Smoothie	Green Protein Powerhouse Smoothie
13	Vanilla Berry Protein Booster Smoothie	Pumpkin Spice Protein Elixir Smoothie	Raspberry Coconut Cream Smoothie
14	Pistachio Banana Cream Smoothie	Strawberry Basil Protein Smoothie	Vanilla Date Cinnamon Cream Smoothie

DAYS	BREAKFAST	LUNCH	DINNER
15	Banana Protein Power House Smoothie	Chocolate Avocado Hemp Elixir Smoothie	Mango Lentil Protein Punch Smoothie
16	Blueberry Almond Burst Smoothie	Chickpea Spinach Smoothie	Chocolate Avocado Dream Smoothie
17	Vanilla Berry Blast Smoothie	Raspberry Coconut Cashew Smoothie	Pistachio Banana Cream Smoothie
18	Pineapple Coconut Smoothie	Sweet Potato and Almond Smoothie	Black Bean and Berry Fusion Smoothie
19	Strawberry Banana Nut Smoothie	Mango Avocado Turmeric Boost Smoothie	Fig Pistachio Cream Dream Smoothie

DAYS	BREAKFAST	LUNCH	DINNER
20	Cherry Almond Butter Elixir Smoothie	Raspberry Almond Quinoa Smoothie	Blueberry Almond Kale Twist Smoothie
21	Apple Cinnamon Roll Smoothie	Nutty Banana Bread Smoothie	Vanilla Date Cinnamon Cream Smoothie
22	Peanut Butter Banana Nut Smoothie	Mango Pistachio Smoothie	Chocolate Avocado Hemp Elixir Smoothie
23	Banana Walnut Butterscotch Smoothie	Strawberry Basil Protein Smoothie	Pineapple Chia Protein Smoothie
24	Raspberry Pistachio Smoothie	Kiwi Hemp Protein Smoothie	Mango Coconut Protein Smoothie

DAYS	BREAKFAST	LUNCH	DINNER
25	Blueberry Almond Smoothie	Caramel Pecan Smoothie	Spinach Walnut Protein Green Goddess Smoothie
26	Berry Quinoa Protein Boost Smoothie	Chocolate Avocado Dream Smoothie	Green Protein Powerhouse Smoothie
27	Vanilla Berry Protein Booster Smoothie	Pumpkin Spice Protein Elixir Smoothie	Raspberry Coconut Cream Smoothie
28	Pistachio Banana Cream Smoothie	Strawberry Basil Protein Smoothie	Vanilla Date Cinnamon Cream Smoothie
29	Banana Protein Power House Smoothie	Chocolate Avocado Hemp Elixir Smoothie	Mango Lentil Protein Punch Smoothie
30	Blueberry Almond Burst Smoothie	Chickpea Spinach Smoothie	Chickpea Spinach Smoothie

4 WEEKS WEIGHT GAIN EXERCISE PLAN

Remember to listen to your body, stay hydrated, and ensure adequate nutrition and rest for recovery. Adjust the weights and intensity based on your fitness level and progression. If you're new to exercise, it's advisable to consult with a fitness professional or healthcare provider before starting a new workout routine.

Day 1-5: Full Body Strength Training

Warm-Up (5-10 minutes)
- Light cardio (jogging, jumping jacks).
- Dynamic stretches (arm circles, leg swings

Strength Training (3 sets x 10-12 reps):
- Squats
- Bench Press
- Bent-Over Rows
- Overhead Press
- Deadlifts

Accessory Exercises (2 sets x 12-15 reps):
- Lunges
- Lat Pulldowns
- Bicep Curls
- Tricep Dips
- Plank (Hold for 30-60 seconds)

Day 6: Rest or Light Activity

Day 7: Active Recovery
- Light activities like walking, yoga, or swimming to promote recovery.

Day 8-12: Upper Body Emphasis

Warm-Up (5-10 minutes)
- Light cardio.
- Dynamic stretches.
-

Upper Body Strength Training (3 sets x 10-12 reps):
- Bench Press
- Overhead Press
- Bent-Over Rows
- Pull-Ups (assisted if needed)
- Dumbbell Curls
- Tricep Pushdowns

Accessory Exercises (2 sets x 12-15 reps):

- Face Pulls
- Hammer Curls
- Tricep Dips
- Plank (Hold for 30-60 seconds)

Day 13: Rest or Light Activity

Day 14: Active Recovery

Day 15-19: Lower Body Emphasis

Warm-Up (5-10 minutes):

- Light cardio.
- Dynamic stretches.

Lower Body Strength Training (3 sets x 10-12 reps):

- Squats
- Deadlifts
- Lunges
- Leg Press
- Leg Curls
- Calf Raises

Accessory Exercises (2 sets x 12-15 reps):

- Hip Thrusts
- Bulgarian Split Squats
- Seated Leg Press
- Plank (Hold for 30-60 seconds)

Day 20: Rest or Light Activity

Day 21: Active Recovery

Day 22-26: Full Body Strength Training with Variation

Warm-Up (5-10 minutes):

- Light cardio.
- Dynamic stretches.

Full Body Strength Training (3 sets x 10-12 reps):
- Squats
- Bench Press
- Bent-Over Rows
- Overhead Press
- Deadlifts

Accessory Exercises (2 sets x 12-15 reps):
- Lunges
- Lat Pulldowns
- Bicep Curls
- Tricep Dips
- Plank (Hold for 30-60 seconds)

Day 27: Rest or Light Activity

Day 28: Active Recovery

Day 29-30: Intense Full Body Strength Training

Warm-Up (5-10 minutes):
- Light cardio.
- Dynamic stretches.

Full Body Strength Training (4 sets x 8-10 reps):
- Squats
- Bench Press
- Bent-Over Rows
- Overhead Press
- Deadlifts

Accessory Exercises (3 sets x 10-12 reps):
- Lunges
- Lat Pulldowns
- Bicep Curls
- Tricep Dips
- Plank (Hold for 30-60 seconds)

CHAPTER 8

Answers to frequently asked questions regarding smoothie weight gain

Here are some often-asked questions about smoothie weight gain:

Can I put on weight only by drinking smoothies?

Although consuming smoothies on their own may not result in weight gain, it can be a simple and enjoyable approach to increasing your calorie consumption.

It's crucial to eat a balanced, nutrient-dense diet, exercise regularly, and be patient and persistent with your weight gain objectives if you want to gain weight healthily and sustainably.

Are there any ingredients that might help me gain weight faster?

Many foods may make you consume more calories and gain weight more quickly. They consist of full-fat dairy products, nut butters, avocados, and fruits like bananas and mangoes.

Not all calories, however, are made equal, so it's crucial to concentrate on eating nutrient-dense meals that provide a mix of protein, healthy fats, and complex carbs.

How often should I consume smoothies to gain weight?

How often you should consume smoothies to acquire weight is a personal decision based on your requirements and objectives. Yet, including smoothies in your diet regularly may be a great strategy to increase your calorie consumption and encourage weight gain.

It's critical to keep in mind the importance of eating a healthy, nutrient-dense diet, exercising often, and being persistent and patient with your weight gain objectives.

How much weight can smoothies help you gain?

Your present weight, height, age, gender, degree of exercise, and calorie consumption are just a few of the variables that will determine how much weight you may reasonably acquire while consuming smoothies.

Smoothies may provide a significant number of calories handily and deliciously, making them a useful tool for weight gain.

It's crucial to remember that weight growth should take place healthily and sustainably rather than ingesting too many calories from unwholesome sources.

You must eat more calories than your body expends to acquire weight. Your specific requirements and objectives will determine the precise quantity of calories you need to eat.

But, as a general rule of thumb, you must eat 3,500 more calories every day to acquire one pound of weight. Smoothies might be a good method to increase your calorie intake.

You may easily add several hundred more calories to your diet by including calorie-dense items such as nut butter, avocado, full-fat dairy, and fruits like bananas or mangoes.

One cup of whole milk, one banana, and two spoonfuls of almond butter, for instance, may provide a smoothie with between 500 and 600 calories.

You may reasonably anticipate gaining 1-2 pounds each week if you follow a balanced diet and include smoothies in your weight-growth regimen.

This pace of weight increase is regarded as safe and sustainable. It's crucial to remember that the precise quantity of weight you acquire will depend on your unique situation.

It's also crucial to remember that consuming smoothies by themselves could not be sufficient to increase weight. To promote weight gain, it's vital to regularly participate in strength training exercises in addition to ingesting smoothies high in calories.

You may guarantee that the weight you acquire is muscle rather than fat by consistently lifting weights or working out with your body weight.

Your requirements and objectives, as well as your eating and activity habits, all have a role in how much weight you may acquire with smoothies.

You may gain weight healthily and sustainably by including calorie-dense ingredients in your smoothies and exercising often. Yet, it's crucial to keep in mind that gaining weight is a slow process that calls for endurance, consistency, and a sensible combination of exercise and diet.

When it comes to weight gain, can smoothies replace meals?

Smoothies may be used as a meal replacement and as a technique to aid with weight gain. To support weight, gain objectives, it's crucial to make sure the smoothie has a mix of calories and nutrients.

If you want to make a smoothie that may serve as a meal substitute and promote weight gain, think about including the following ingredients:

1.**Protein:** Upping your protein intake and encouraging muscle building by adding protein powder or Greek yogurt to your smoothie might help you gain weight. Whey protein powder, soy protein, and pea protein are all excellent sources of protein.

2. **Healthy Fats:** Good fats may assist improve calorie intake and provide the body energy. Examples include avocado, nut butter, and coconut oil. Also essential for hormone synthesis, cell development, and organ defense are fats.

3. **Oats, sweet potatoes, and fruits** like bananas and mangoes are examples of complex carbs that may both give you energy and make you feel full. Due to their slow digestion, complex carbs may maintain blood sugar levels and avoid energy slumps.

4.**Nutrient-Dense Add-Ins:** Using nutrient-dense items may provide vitamins and minerals that are crucial for general health and well-being, such as spinach, kale, or berries.

These components may also provide antioxidants and anti-inflammatory substances, which can aid in post-exercise recovery and guard against free radical damage.

5.It's crucial to consider **portion sizes and calorie consumption** while making a meal replacement smoothie for weight gain.

A meal replacement smoothie may include anywhere from 400 to 800 calories, depending on calorie demands.

To maintain a balance of nutrients and advance general health, it's also crucial to eat a range of meals throughout the day.

Although smoothies might aid in weight growth and serve as a meal substitute, they shouldn't be the only source of nourishment.

For long-term health and sustained weight growth, a balanced, diversified diet that includes a range of complete foods is essential. Regular exercise, especially strength training, is crucial for boosting weight growth and the development of muscle.

Can you increase your muscle mass with smoothies?

Smoothies may be a delightful and simple method to eat a balanced combination of nutrients that assist muscle building, making them a useful tool for supporting muscle gain.

Use items that provide the ideal ratio of protein, carbs, and healthy fats when making smoothies for muscle growth.

To grow and repair muscles, protein is a necessary macronutrient, thus it's crucial to include a source of protein in your smoothie. Greek yogurt, nut butter, and whey protein powder are all excellent sources of protein. Strive for a smoothie with at least 20 to 30 grams of protein.

During exercise, carbohydrates may assist muscles in recovering by refueling their glycogen reserves. Oats, sweet potatoes, and fruits like bananas and berries are examples of complex carbs that help maintain energy levels and aid in muscle rehabilitation.

Avocados, almonds, and coconut oil are examples of healthy fats that may assist improve calorie intake and provide the body with energy. Also essential for hormone synthesis, cell development, and organ defense are fats.

It's crucial to consume nutrient-dense supplements like spinach, kale, or berries along with these macronutrients since they provide vitamins and minerals that are crucial for general health and well-being.

Also, these substances may include anti-inflammatory and antioxidant components that aid in supporting post-exercise recovery and guard against free radical damage.

Although smoothies might aid in muscle growth, it's crucial to remember that they shouldn't be the only source of nutrients. For long-term health and sustained muscle building, a balanced, diverse diet that includes a range of nutritious foods is essential.

Progressive loading and frequent strength training are important techniques for gaining muscle hypertrophy.

It's crucial to consider portion sizes and calorie consumption while utilizing smoothies to grow muscle. A muscle-building smoothie may include anything from 400 to 800 calories, depending on calorie demands.

To maintain a balance of nutrients and advance general health, it's also crucial to eat a range of meals throughout the day.

How to adapt to your smoothie consumption when your weight fluctuates?

It's crucial to modify your smoothie consumption as you lose or gain weight to maintain your nutritional requirements and progress toward your health objectives.

<u>**The following advice can help you regulate your smoothie consumption when your weight fluctuates:**</u>

1.Identify your new calorie requirements: Your calorie requirements will alter as you put on or lose weight. To make sure you are getting enough calories to support your health objectives, it's crucial to frequently reassess your caloric requirements. Determine your new calorie requirements by using an internet calculator or talking to a trained nutritionist.

2.Change the amounts you eat: Increase or decrease the portion sizes of your smoothies following your new calorie requirements.

You may need to increase the smoothie portion sizes if you're aiming to gain weight. You may need to reduce the smoothie serving amounts if you're attempting to lose weight.

3.Change the ratios of your macronutrients: You may need to modify the smoothies' macronutrient ratios based on your weight-loss objectives.

You may need to consume more protein and good fats if you're attempting to put on weight. You may need to eat fewer carbs and fats if you're attempting to reduce weight.

4.Add nutrient-dense ingredients: It's vital to include nutrient-dense additions like spinach, kale, or berries in your smoothies whether you're attempting to gain weight or lose it. These components provide essential vitamins and minerals for general health and well-being.

5.Keep an eye on how your body reacts: Pay attention to how your body reacts as you alter the number of smoothies you consume. You may need to further modify your intake if you are not getting the desired outcomes.

You could need to change the smoothie's components if any unfavourable side effects, including bloating or digestive discomfort, are happening to you. But keep in mind that smoothies are one element of a balanced diet.

To make sure that you are fulfilling your nutritional requirements and advancing your health objectives, it's crucial to eat a range of healthy foods. Regular exercise, especially strength training, is crucial for supporting weight control and developing muscle.

To choose the right diet and exercise routine for you, speak with a licensed dietitian or other healthcare professionals.

CONCLUSION

Smoothies are a great way to get a range of nutrients in one serving while also adding convenience and flavour to your diet. Smoothies may be made to suit your specific requirements and tastes, whether you're trying to put on weight, lose weight, or keep it off.

Smoothies provide an easy method to get a lot of calories in one serving, making them particularly beneficial for anyone trying to gain weight. You can simply add calories to your smoothies by adding calorie-dense items like nuts, seeds, and nut butters.

But, it's crucial to remember that smoothies shouldn't be your only source of nutrients. It's crucial to eat a range of complete foods and supplements to promote general health and wellbeing and to make sure that you are getting all the nutrients you need each day.

To promote general health and wellbeing, it's crucial to keep in mind that smoothies should be consumed in addition to a balanced diet and regular exercise.